Honesty in the Bible

written by
Sunny Kang

illustrated by
Alexandro Ockyno

Text and Illustrations Copyright © 2021 Sunny Kang
All rights reserved. No part of this publication may be reproduced, distributed, or transmitted in any form or by any means, including photocopying, recording, or other electronic or mechanical methods, without the prior written permission of the publisher, except in the case of brief quotations embodied in reviews and certain other non-commercial uses permitted by copyright law. The moral right of the author and illustrator has been asserted.
Cover design and illustrations by Alexandro Ockyno

E-Book: 978-1-7363548-9-6
Paperback: 978-1-7378681-0-1
Hardcover: 978-1-7378681-1-8

Speak TRUTH in love and set many people FREE!

To :

From :

Date :

What is Honesty?

Honesty is telling the truth even when it is not easy.

Moses

"And Moses was instructed in all the wisdom of the Egyptians, and he was mighty in his words and deeds."

-Acts 7:22-

Baby Moses was born in a time when the Israelites were slaves in Egypt. The ruler of Egypt at the time, Pharaoh, was afraid of the Israelites growing too much. Since he was afraid, he wanted no more Israelite, or Hebrew, baby boys in Egypt.

However, at three months old,
baby Moses was placed in a basket and sent down a river.
He was found by Pharaoh's daughter and raised by Moses' mother!
Raised in Pharaoh's house, Moses grew up as royalty.

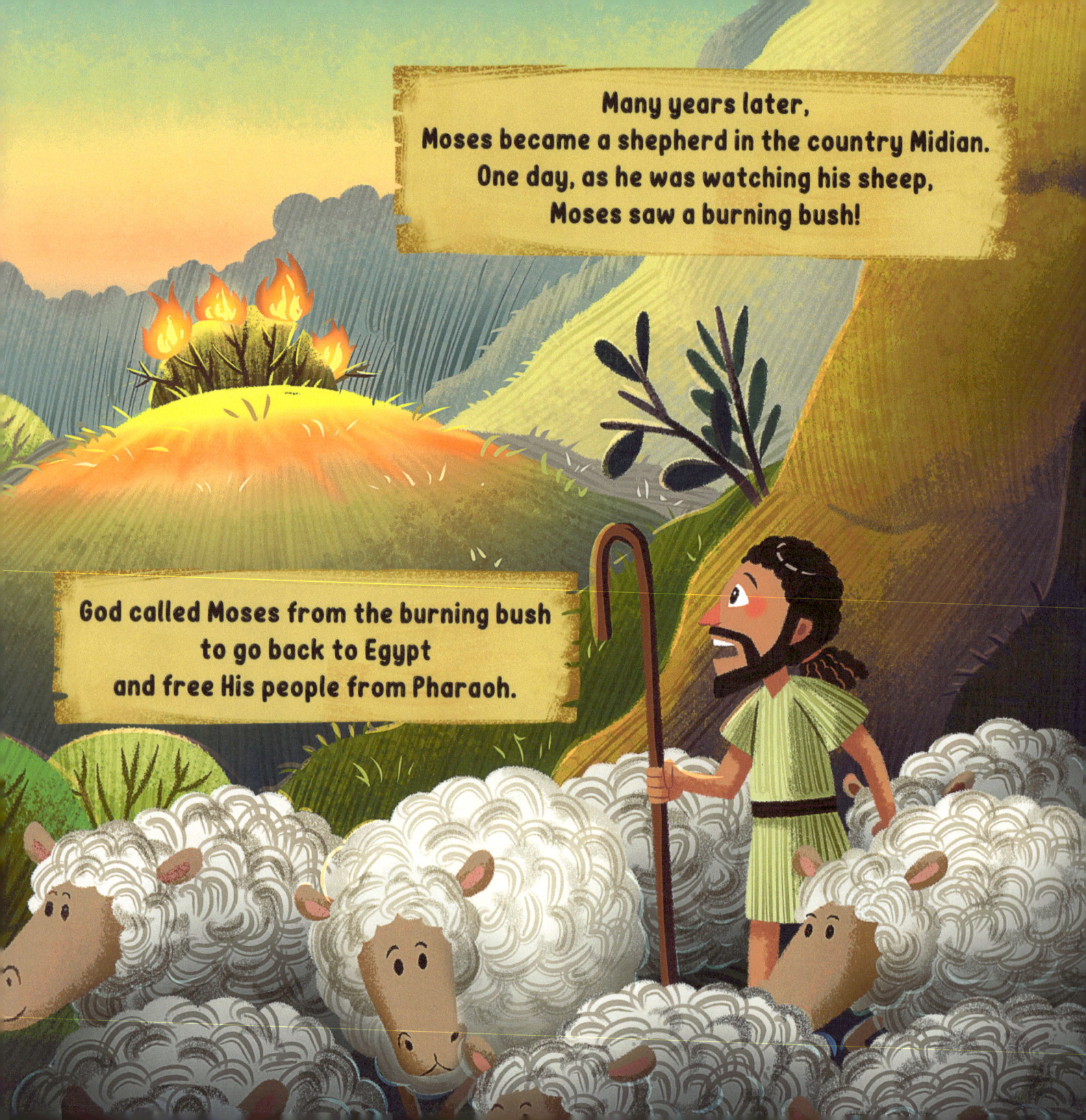

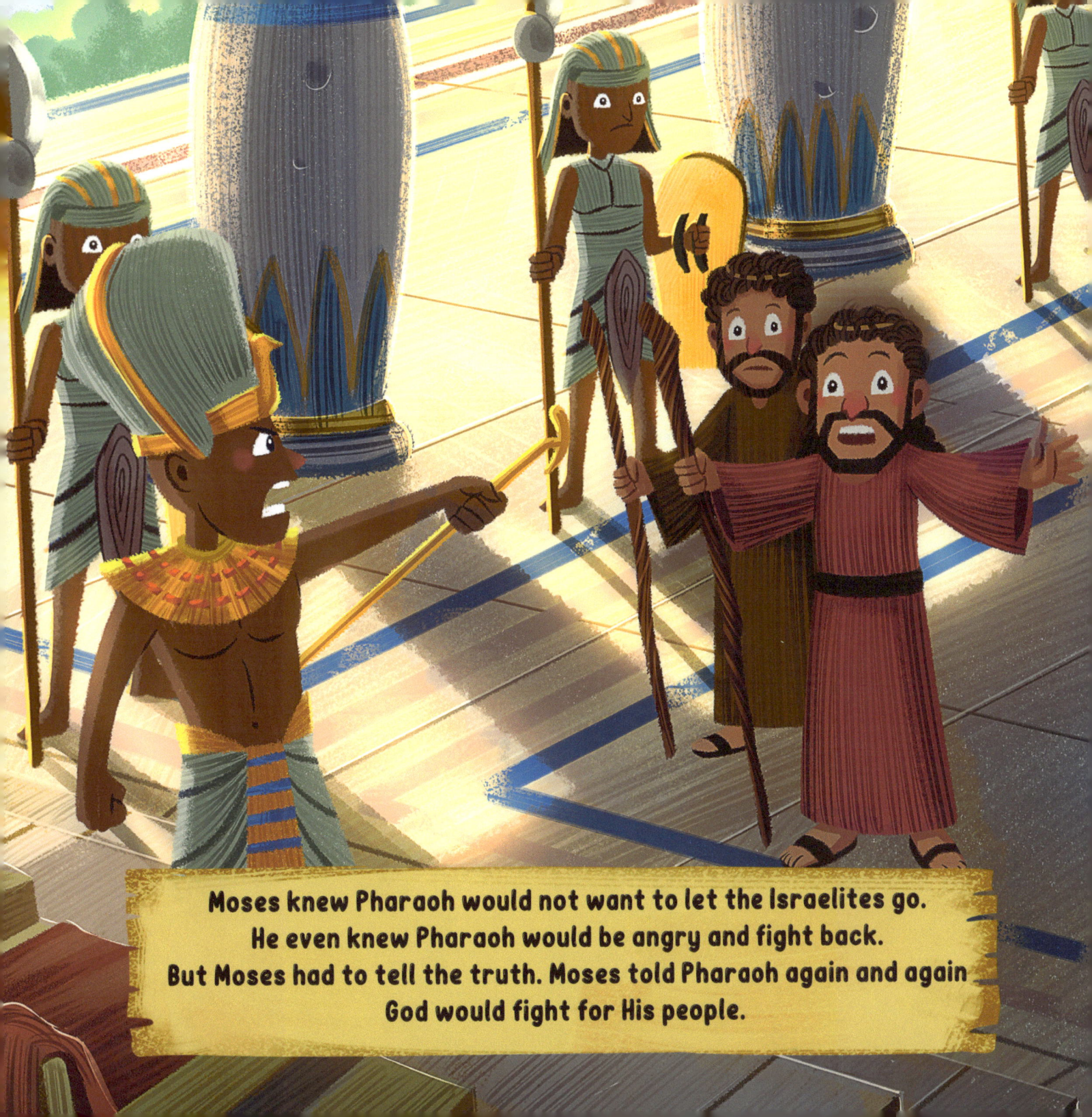

Moses knew Pharaoh would not want to let the Israelites go. He even knew Pharaoh would be angry and fight back. But Moses had to tell the truth. Moses told Pharaoh again and again God would fight for His people.

John the Baptist

In those days
John the Baptist came preaching in the wilderness of Judea,
"Repent, for the kingdom of heaven is at hand."
-Matthew 3:1-2-

The angel Gabriel announced the birth of John the Baptist to his father, Zechariah.
His mother, Elizabeth, also knew her son's name was to be John.

John grew up to be a mighty man of God.
He preached and baptized many people in the wilderness.
People from all over came to hear him speak the truth.

Being honest and speaking the truth was not always easy though. He told the people they must believe God and do good works. If they don't do both, they would hurt themselves and others.

Stephen

And Stephen, full of grace and power,
was doing great wonders and signs among the people.

-Acts 6:8-

After Jesus rose from the dead and ascended into heaven, Jesus sent the Holy Spirit to His disciples to be pure and powerful. This was the start of the church.

When Stephen was asked to tell the truth, he was very honest.
He told the truth about God being faithful to Abraham, Jacob, and Joseph.
He told the truth about Moses and God freeing the Israelites from Pharaoh.
He talked about God loving King David and King Solomon.

And finally, Stephen told them how many people hurt the prophets who spoke God's Word, especially Jesus Christ.
The people became so mad at Stephen,
but Stephen saw Jesus standing to welcome him to heaven!

Paul

Paul, a servant of Christ Jesus,
called to be an apostle,
set apart for the gospel of God.

-Romans 1:1-

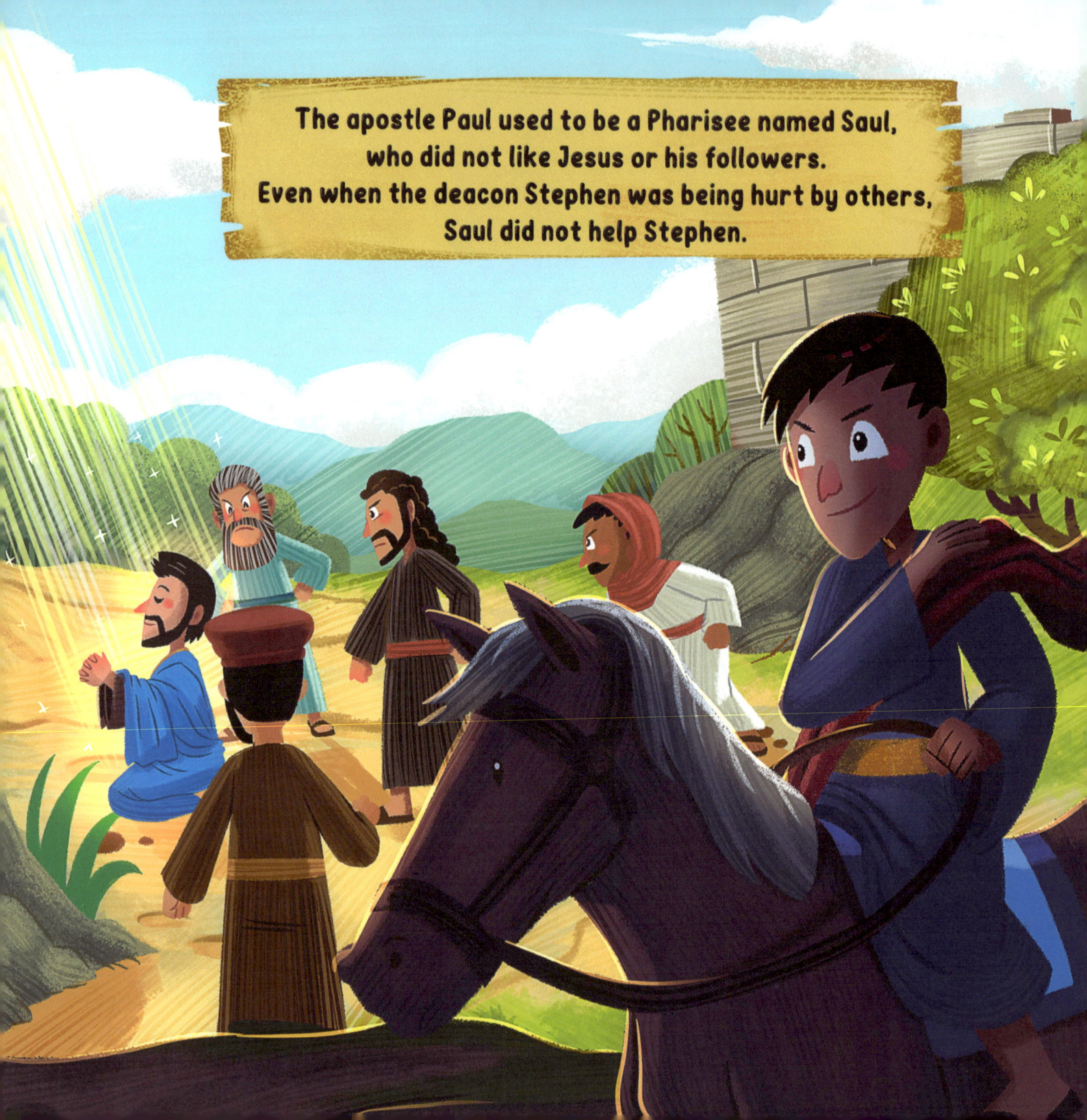

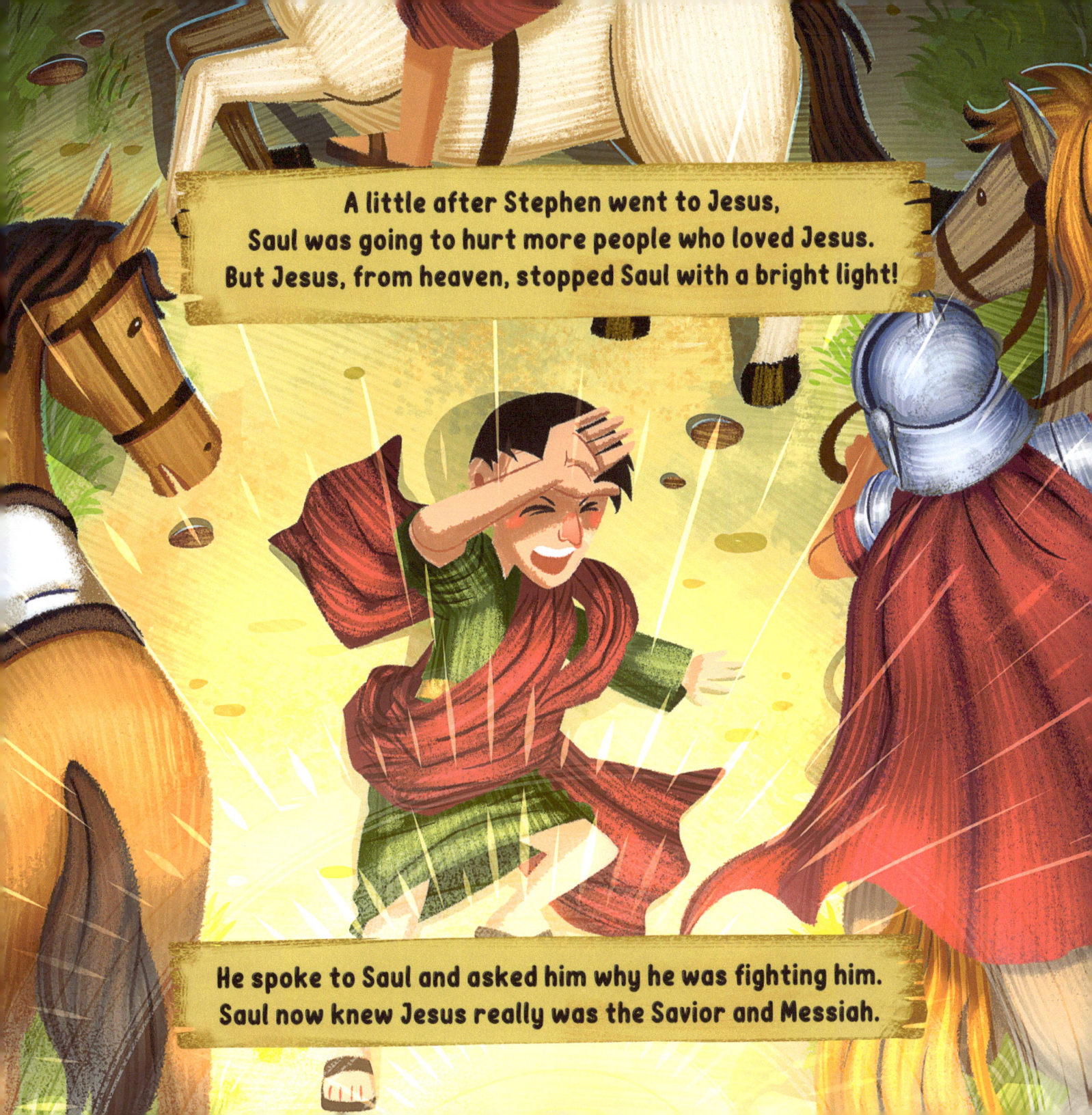

Paul shared his story with many people.
He shared how he once was lost, but now is found.
He once hated Jesus, but Jesus loved him
and changed him for good.

Jesus

I [Jesus] am the way, the truth, and the life.
No one comes to the Father except through me.
-John 14:6-

Since Jesus was young, he was always honest and loving. He was full of grace and truth.

When he became older and started to preach and teach, people were amazed by the power of His words. He did not try to make everyone happy or to like Him. He spoke the truth because truth sets people free.

Jesus was even honest when he said he would die one day and rise again in three days. When the disciples saw Jesus come alive again, they were amazed and followed him again!

How Can We Be More Honest?

Ask Jesus into your heart!
Believe everything Jesus says!
Choose to follow Him every day!

Do you believe in Jesus as your Savior and lifelong leader?

About the Author and Illustrator

Author
Sunny Kang is a Christ follower, husband, father, teacher, preacher, and author. He has pastored for over 10 years, serving as children's pastor for several of those years. He enjoys learning, meeting new people, communicating God's Word, superhero movies, and boba! He, his wife, and 2 sons live and serve in Las Vegas.

Follow Author:
Facebook: @AuthorSunnyKang
Instagram: @AuthorSunnyKang
Newsletter: http://bit.ly/authorsunnykang

Illustrator
Alexandro Ockyno is a full time freelance illustrator, living in Bali for almost 9 years. A happy man with a beautiful girlfriend, his dream is to create many children's books and share God's blessings with many others.

Follow Illustrator:
Facebook: @alessandro.altobelly
Instagram: @catandsashimi

Thank you
and hope you enjoyed this 2nd book
in the "Seeds to Trees" series!

DOWNLOAD YOUR FREE GIFT HERE!

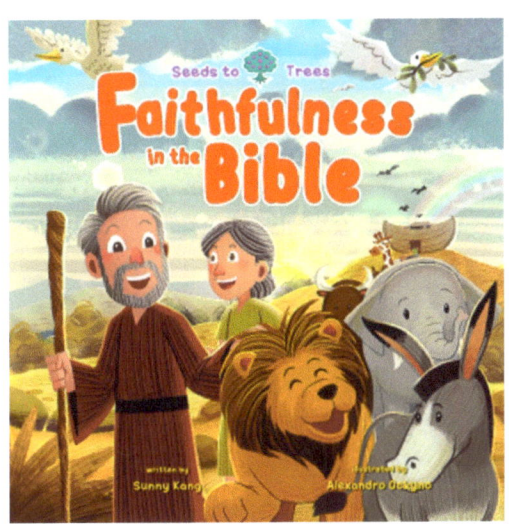

Link: https://bit.ly/Faithfulness-In-The-Bible